Mairéad Byrne's poems are mov of observation and playful imagination fuse with the minutiae of daily life to create small missives of quirky and insightful documentation. Her source material includes everything from the weather to credit card bills to news reports to human body parts to animal pelts and all of these seemingly disparate details amass into a kind of living, breathing envelope that holds the marrow of existence itself in all its harsh reality, weird surreality, absurdity, fragility, and occasional beauty. Often funny and sometimes sobering, Byrne's work exposes the difficult-to-reconcile distractions, detritus, and rubble that surround us from all sides, but also culls glowing artifacts from such debris.
Juliet Cook

A modest ma(s)terwork of colors & delights, of plays of language (lost & found), the push & pull of parody, of politics & domesticities, of day to day conundrums, of observations & inventions, of the connection (as she has it) of "small things to other small things," of the oft-derided fancy as the brighter sister of imagination. These are some thoughts that flash by while reading Mairéad Byrne's agile, humoristic, & deceptively profound new book. The best of, surely, & with a promise of still more to come.
Jerome Rothenberg

heaven

and then some

- something to look forward to.
Murphy Chang

The Best of (What's Left of) *Heaven*

Publishing Genius
2200 Maryland Ave C1
Baltimore, MD 21218
www.publishinggenius.com

Cover design by Stephanie Barber
www.stephaniebarber.com

Printed on recycled paper

ISBN 13: 978-0-9820813-5-8
ISBN 10: 0-9820813-5-9

The Best of (What's Left of) *Heaven*

Mairéad Byrne

Publishing Genius
Baltimore, MD

to the margins

CONTENTS

People don't get no time to feel and spend them intelligence. The most intelligent ... and innocent are poor, are crumbled and get brutalized. Daily.
Bob Marley

Thursday, January 01, 2004
Dammit more champagne.

Friday, January 02, 2004
Dammit no more champagne.

LIGHT IN FEBRUARY

gold
golden
rose-gold
light gold light blue

light-grey
grey
high bright blue
golden-blue
blue-golden

transparent light blue
blue-time
bright grey
calm grey
grey w/ light blue notes
grey/foggy
lucid grey
high cold blue-sunny
light-blue-sunny

blue-silver-gold
grey-moist
blue-gold

blue-gold-cold
yellow-blue
white-grey-cold
golden blue-snowing
yellow-blue-cold
blue-gold

grey-white-cold

SPRING

March
March
March
March
March
March
March
March
March
March
March
March
March
March
March
March
March
March
March
March
March
March
March
March
March
March
March
March
March
March
March
april

light in april

                                    dull grey
                      irish rain

                bluey   warm
         silver-grey tarnished silver

                sunny golden white gold
                         light blue silve
      warm golden   tarnished silv

   golden-blue   sunny   golde

        light grey light

     grey-white   leaf green
                       leaf-green

      golden-blue
        peaks blue-light-gold
        silver-grey   light leaf
        gold & silver-blue
            grey, lowering

gold

      golden

old   balmy blue
  gloomy
            gloomy rain-tarnished stars
ellow-green

   light green & grey

& white-gold
  light blue   green-blue

       sublime
  green & light blue

from THE WEATHER

5.1.04
A glorious May Day in Providence; dusty inside.
5.2.04
A rainy May day in Providence. I wanted to write a paean to May this morning before I set foot outside. But the fact is: there are magnolia blossoms all over the ground tonight, & Fall is in the air.
5.3.04
A rainy May day in Providence, coldish.
5.4.04
Just about jacketless day in Providence.
5.5.04
I suppose there was (May) weather today in Providence.
5.6.04
I think it was sunny today in Providence.
5.7.04
A sunny day in Providence, easy, no coat.
5.8.04
A fine sunny day in Providence.
5.9.04
A rainy day in Providence, sun towards evening.
5.10.04
A sunny breezy day in Providence.
5.11.04
A warm breezy day in Providence.
5.12.04
A very warm sunny day in Providence.
5.13.04
Overcast in the morning; then a sparkling day in Providence.
5.14.04
Overcast & coldish in the morning, then sunny & calm in Providence.
5.15.04
A lovely sunny day in Providence, very warm but heavenly toward evening.

5.16.04

A very beautiful, sunny day in Providence; rain in the morning.

5.17.04

A cooler, overcast day in Providence.

5.18.04

An easy day in Providence.

5.19.04

Clio & I stepped in grey calm this morning; a very easy day in Providence.

5.20.04

A sunny warm day in Providence; teaching & in the office; payday.

5.21.04

A sublime evening in Providence, though cold & grey in the morning.
Last class at last.

5.22.04

A coldish grey day in Providence.

5.23.04

A grey rainy day in Providence, coldish, green trees, russet brick.

5.24.04

Cold hands this morning; no car; at last sun towards evening in Providence.

5.25.04

A coldish day in Providence, threatening rain.

5.26.04

Another gloomy grey day in Providence, & cold. What's happening?

5.27.04

At last the sun comes out in Providence.

5.28.04

Back in the doldrums today, rain, greyness, luxury of staying at home
for some of it.

5.29.04

Sunny at last (all day) in Providence.

5.30.04

A beautiful sunny day in Providence, blowy.

5.31.04

A greyish day in Providence.

STATE HOUSE, JUNE

brush stroke against stipple
moth-wing against paint
[despair against nonchalance]
blur against comprehension
blur on haze
sigh against pillow
wrinkled bedsheet on cloud hammock
skein against wool
old silver against glass pane
chamois against old iron
chipped cup among cloud suds
vanilla ice against perfect blue
polished white against smoky blue
soft blue against pale sky
soft flame against apricot froth
incandescence against varicose blue
bluish white against old rose
dove breast against blue veil
glance against equanimity
ash against white ash
dust on milk
chalk smear on grey screen
grey breast against blue sky
beacon against purple swathe
pearl drop on bruised mantle
yellow cream against fog
[yellow cream against spray]
[sobriety against morning]
[blessing against finality]
[old head on stark pillow]

SUMMER HOURS

At sundown men in loose powder-blue overalls come in a white city truck and unfurl tarps stashed between the bars of the wrought-iron fence and nudge them up and out over the park occluding the darkening saturated sky, making a sky beneath the sky, a darker place through which they feel their way back, by smell, by touch, to the edge, where they hang briefly, more audible than visible, before zipping the park up for the night, piling into the truck and driving away.

AUGUST

August so much deserves its name. It is August: *Inspiring awe or admiration; majestic. Venerable because of age or rank.* Let's not make those tough choices I say: *Inspiring awe **and** admiration*, why not. *Majestic* August, morning after morning drawing back the curtains on your throne-room of sun. Some days your hand spices heavy, some days soporific, some days you throw gems sparking our drowse into sharp corners, humming-birds shaving that millimeter from anything grown mossy, buffing mold, spinning air into tiny fresh windmills. *Venerable because of age*—of course. How long have you been going on? You demon. Somehow having smuggled at least one hundred sunny days into this one month no-one dreams to ask how old you are. You are so lateral. Such a horizontality. And *rank*. Well yes. The marigolds are giving up the ghost. Some leaves chalky white. Or balled pathetically. If it were wetter, it would be true rank. Eighth mobster. As it is, you could say sometimes: *Botanic Gardens*, sometimes *hothouse*, sometimes *musky*, sometimes *rot*, sometimes *what a glorious day*. All month my *American Heritage Dictionary* has lain open on its Norwegian cloth on a Wal-Mart table by the window in our sunshiny upstairs hall. Perceptibly the house has gotten cleaner, tidier, *more pulled together* as they say in teen magazines. My dictionary lies open absorbing motes. If it could see, it would see, out of the corners of its pages, just beyond view, *recuperation*, steadily.

STATE HOUSE, SEPTEMBER

candle-flame against turquoise
pearl against lavender
mint against rose
breast-milk on mauve
metal against mackerel
yellowed lace on watered silk
graphite on glass
silhouette on pale blue
eggshell on streaked blue
grey cut-out against sky-blue
velcro on azure
cupped flame on indigo
old snow on cerulean
gravestone on cobalt
sepulchre white against Ascension Day cloud
mausoleum white against Renaissance cloud
light slate against milky cloud
soft white on white
dove-grey against white
old bone against smoke
thumbprint in smoke
dead bone on dirty wool
haze on fog
lemon pith on light grey
ivory on blue-grey
rosé against blue-grey
spooky grey on grey
graphite on glass
mauve against ash
shadow on shade

FALL

Now when I come home at night
I take my pate off
& watch the gold & auburn trees
surge & blow

STATE HOUSE, NOVEMBER

blur against haze
slate against glaze
[fuzz against gauze]
calm against calm
ash against cloud
milk against cup
[palm against brow]
bone against flux
wet newsprint on flock
web against sheen
hemp against smoke
lit paper about to explode
thumbnail against lens
smudge against lens
lens against cloud downsweep
faint green on cloud tumble
grass stain against apricot
stance against drift
incipience against skepticism
biscuit against cornflower
powdered stone against metal
ink surge in tumbler
pale gold against inky cloud
[pallor against slab]
pallor against oblivion
back against wall
something against nothing
vertical against horizontal
fingertip against nape
touch against skin

SYSTEM RESTORE

I couldn't stand Christmas anymore.
I had to go out.
It was raining.
I didn't bring an umbrella.
My boots leaked.
It was great.
I could write poetry again.

a car

nosing out
at a funny angle
w/o a driver

is probably just a
car

backing out

SIGN

Fresh today!
Wild Fries!
Caught & Squashed This Morning!
Giant Fries!

SLEEP!

Free of charge!
Luxury item!
In your own home!
In-flight movies!
No skills needed!
Be your own boss!
Better than sex!
No calories!
Fat-free!

PULLING INTO NYC THROUGH THE BRONX & ON BONANZA BUS

I could be them!
I could be with them!
I could be her!
I could be with him!
I could have gloves!
I wish I was them!
I wish I was with them!
I wish I was rushing to church or X's place!
This is just like when—
Remembering when—
NYC I must live one of my 9 lives in you!
NYC with all my lovers!
My agents!
My funnest friends & laughing audiences!
My familiar indecipherables!

LEARNING TO RIDE
THE BICYCLE OF MY LIFE

I'm doing it!
I'm doing it!
I'm doing it!
I'm doing it!
I'm doing it!
I'm doing it!
I'M DOING IT!!!

A DIFFERENT KIND OF RHYME

A Family That Prays Together Prays Together.
A Family That Stays Together Stays Together.

A Stitch In Time Saves Time.
A Friend In Need Is A Friend In Need.

Early To Bed & Early To Rise Makes A Man Early To Bed & Early To Rise.
Might Is Might.
No Pain No Pain.

MORE INTERESTING RHYMES

Business Is Business.
Fight Fire With Fire.
First Things First.
Let Bygones Be Bygones.
What's Done Is Done.

LUDDITE

I'm no Luddite.
I just like saying *Luddite*.

LIEDER

Sp—re—eh—chen—Sie—Deu—tsch—sch—sch?
Eh—eh—del—weiss
Ei—ei—ne—kl—ei—ein—eh na—ah—ah—AH-ACHT—MUS-IK!
Ko—o—oh—m—m—men SIE Hi—er
LANG—SAM LANG—SAM
Sch—Neh—eh—LL—ER!
Ein je—eh—de—er ENG—el ist SCHRECK—lich—ch—ch—sssshhhhh
Auf—Wie—e—e—e—der—SEH-en
Ge—SUN—UN—UN—UN—D—h—h—h—EIT!

OATMEAL SONG

Give me an oatmeal bath
Come take an oatmeal bath with me
Oatmeal dry or wet
Oatmeal makes you free

Oatmeal
Oatmeal
Oatmeal
Oatmeal
Oatmeal

I will knit you an oatmeal sweater
I will knit you a sweater of oatmeal

When you go to college
I will knit you an oatmeal sweatshirt

I kid you not!
I kid you not!

[Chorus]

Oatmeal
Oatmeal
Oatmeal
Oatmeal
Oatmeal

We will live in an oatmeal land
I will read you oatmeal books
We will wallow in oatmeal baths
Oatmeal will be our bed

& when the time comes
To bury you, my love
I will bury you in oatmeal
In oatmeal I will bury you

Oatmeal
Oatmeal
Oatmeal
Oatmeal
Oatmeal

[Repeat chorus]

Come to the oatmeal gate
Down the winding oatmeal road
Come see the sun set in its oatmeal bowl
Come see the rise of the oatmeal moon
My love

Oatmeal!
Oatmeal!

Words by Aurelius Plimp
Arr. Marcella Turf-Maguire

SOUL SONG FOR 10 PEOPLE

So what I say to myself is
No matter what happens
We got each other
We're in this together
Oh you're leaving?
Oh okay

What I say to myself is
No matter what happens
We got each other
We're in this together
Oh you're leaving
Oh okay

What I say to myself is
No matter what happens
We got each other
We're in this together
Oh you're leaving?
Oh okay

What I say to myself is
No matter what happens
We got each other
We're in this together
Oh you're leaving
Oh okay

What I say to myself is
No matter what happens
We got each other
We're in this together
Oh you're leaving?
Oh okay

What I say to myself is
No matter what happens
We got each other
We're in this together
Oh you're leaving
Oh okay

What I say to myself is
No matter what happens
We got each other
We're in this together
Oh you're leaving?
Oh okay

What I say to myself is
No matter what happens
We're in this together
We got each other
Oh you're leaving
Oh okay

What I say to myself is
No matter what happens
We got each other
We're in this together
You're leaving?
Oh

NERVES

The leg of the table.
Aaaagh!
Light.
Aaaagh!
The image in the frame.
Aaaagh!
The card catalog.
Aaaagh!
Piped music in the bank.
Aaaagh!
Blocky calves that look carved
skeined in black tights.
Aaaaaagh!
The cistern.
Aaaagh!
A knot.
Aaaaagh!
The thought of her hard curls.
Aaaaagh!
Bagpipes.
Aaaaaaaagh!
The time she takes getting to the point.
Aaaagh!
A hair on the soap.
Aaaaagh!
A fly in the bag!
Aaaaagh!
The thought of a fly in the bag.
Aaaaaaaaagh!
A tangled cord.

Aaaagh!
Approaching figure blocked by a tree.
Aaaaaaaagh!
The thought of Dickens!
Aaaaaagh!
Arm of glasses sticking out.
Aaaaagh!
Right name for "arm" of glasses.
Aaaaaaagh!
Quotation marks.
Aaaaaaagh!

I HAVE BEEN SO MUCH HAPPIER & MORE AT EASE SINCE I DISCOVERED THE ANSWER TO MOST QUESTIONS IS MONEY

A roof-over-your-head?
Money.
Looking good?
Money.
Time to write?
Money.
Books published?
Money.
Time for the kids?
Money.
Need to get someplace fast?
Money.
Bite to eat?
Money.
Love?
Pass.
Love?
Money.
Kindly relations with your hairdresser?
Money.
Disasters.
Money.
Disease?
Money.
Death?
Well, er … *money?*

I'M EXCITED

Looks like I'll be able to pay my credit card bill!

MISERY

No money in the bank.
Sirens in the air.
Snow on the ground.

ANTIDOTE

Soup.
George Carlin.
Poetry.

MISERY

Thinking of a better joke—
too late.

OKAY,

so which do you care most about—
the bitternesses of the past or say—
your jeans?

I dunno.
I feel pretty strong about
my jeans.

EXPECTING THE MAIL

I refuse to accept that this is the mail:
This is not the mail.

I'm looking forward to the mail!

WOULD YOU

So if you could
would you?

Would you—
if you could?

I mean would you—
if you could?

Would you?

Would you really?

Would you—
if you could?

Would you?

WHERE DID YOU GROW UP?

Do you mean why did I grow up?

No—where did you grow up?

Do you mean how did I grow up?

No—*where* did you grow up?

Do you mean when?

No—just where.

Oh!

YOU NEVER KNOW (*formal*)

You never know.
You never know.
You *never* know.
You never *know*.
You never know.

YOU NEVER KNOW (*loose*)

You never know.
You never really know.
You never really know now do you.
You never know.
You just never know.

YOU NEVER KNOW (*wheedling*)

Ah you never know.
Sure you never know do you.
You never really know.
You never never know.
Isn't that the truth.
You never know.

I DON'T CARE

I don't care.
I don't care.
I *don't* care.
I don't *care*.
I don't care.

I DON'T CARE (*demoralized*)

I don'tcare.
Iduncare.
oin-care.
ncare.
uh.

CRAZY I DONT CARE

I DONT CARE!!!
I!!! DONT!!! CARE!!!
I!!!DONT!!!!CARE!!!!!
!!!!!I DON!!!T CARE!!!!!!
GAAAAAAAAAAAAAAAAAAAAAAAAA

Q & A

Q: Er, guys, could you go a little quieter? It's 5.30am …
A: ARE YOU KIDDING? WE'RE **THE GARBAGE MEN!**

ARE YOU KIDDING ME?

Are YOU kidding me?
Are you KIDDING ME?
Are you kidding me?
Are you kidding me?
ARE you KIDDING me?
Are you *kidding* me?
Are you kidding me?
Are *you* kidding me?
ARE YOU KIDDING ME?

GREEDY

Here—
Here's an hour—
YIKES!

Here—
Here's a day—
YIKES!

Okay here—
I'll pull an all-nighter—
YIKES!!!

Okay here—
Take my whole life
!!!!!!YIKES!!!!!!

GOOD JOKE

Then I took a day off.

Then I'll take a day off.

Then I'll probably take a day off.

Then if there's time I'll take a day off.

Then with a bit of luck I'll take a day off.

Then it would be fantastic if I could take a day off.

Then I'm going to try to take a day off.

Then I'll take half a day off.

What I was thinking of

actually was a cup of

coffee before work

how great is

that

YOU HAVE TO LAUGH

You have to laugh
You have to laugh
Ah you have to laugh
You hafta laugh
You hafta laugh though
Don't you just have to laugh
You hafta laugh
Ah you hafta laugh
You have to laugh
You have to laugh
fuckit

UGLY MAN

UGLY MAN
CALLING
calling
ugly man

coast-to-coast calling
DO YOU READ ME
UGLY MAN

COME IN
UGLY MAN
ugly man
COME IN

ENTHUSIASM

I clapped until little drops of blood
jumped out of my finger.

My life is not large-scale—
but intense.

HOW TO KILL A SQUIRREL & OTHER GAME

To KILL a SQUIRREL heave things at it
To KILL a MONGOOSE—PELLETS
To KILL a SNAKE—USE it as a BELT
To KILL an ELEPHANT—JET bead
To KILL a CHINCHILLA—RAIN
To KILL a GERBIL—PINK PAPER
To KILL a TARANTULA—BLEACH
To SCARE ROBBERS—throw LEMON BARS at them
To DEMOLISH a building—run MARATHON RUNNERS into it
To KILL a CATERPILLAR—catapult
To KILL a SCORPION—COLT 45
To KILL an OCTOPUS—BUCKET of PAINT

TO SKIN A MUSKRAT

First cut the pelt around the tail and all four feet at the fur line. Next cut the pelt from the heel of each hind foot to the anus. Pull the pelt and, by cutting connective tissue where necessary, peel the pelt down from the hind legs and the tail. Cuts will be required to remove the pelt at the ears and eyes. If desired, the carcass can be hung by the hind legs, using a gambrel at a convenient height. Pull the pelt down the carcass as far as it will go, exposing the base of the forelegs. Pass a finger between the foreleg and pelt; then using a push and pull motion, strip the skin from each leg. When both forelegs are free, pull the pelt down the carcass, past the neck to the base of the ears. The head of the carcass should be partially exposed. Locate the cartilage that attaches the ears to the skull and cut as close as possible to the skull. Pull the pelt lower to reveal the connective tissue around the eyes. Cut the tissue close to the skull using a sharp knife. No fur should be left around the ears and eyes. Pull the pelt down again, finally exposing the loose flesh around the lips. Free the pelt from the carcass by cutting around the lips and through the nose cartilage. This is nothing like writing poetry.

TO SKIN A RACCOON

First cut the pelt around the "ankles" and "wrists" where the long fur ends. Next cut the pelt from the heel of each hind foot to the anus and around the anus. Finally cut from the anus straight down the tail about 4 inches. If the raccoon is a male, reproductive organs will be connected to the pelt. These are cut off as close to the pelt as possible. Now peel the pelt from around the base of the tail exposing a couple of inches of the tail bone. Clamp a tail stripper around the tail bone with one hand and hold the base of the tail with your other hand and attempt to pull the tail bone out of the tail by pulling the tail stripper. If the tail bone does not pull out, extend the cut several more inches toward the tip of the tail. Free more of the tail bone from the pelt by cutting the connective tissue and then try to pull the tail bone out. Once the tail bone is pulled, extend the cut on the tail straight to the tip. The pelt should now be pulled down the carcass as far as it will go exposing the forelegs. Further expose the forelegs by cutting the connective tissue. Wrap fingers from both of your hands around the raccoon's foreleg and support it while pushing the pelt down. Keep pushing until the raccoon's forefoot passes through the pelt and the pelt is free. Repeat this process with the other foreleg. As with the muskrat, the ears, eyes, nose and lips should be cut free without leaving any fur on the carcass. As with poetry, all 5 senses are involved.

BOARDING BEAVER

Nail the pelt to heavy plywood, the end of a cable drum, or on some other flat surface in a round or wide oval shape. It helps to have permanently drawn concentric circles or ovals of various sizes marked on the board to serve as a guide when nailing. Be careful not to overstretch the pelt. When finished, the nails should be no more than 1 inch apart. Use nails at least 2 inches long and, once the pelt is nailed up, pull it away from the board up onto the nails so that air can circulate behind it. Pelts can also be sewn onto a hoop frame of metal or wood. The pelt should be sewn loosely using stitches one inch apart. Once it has been attached all the way around, the stitches can be pulled tight all around. Some metal hoops are adjustable and the stitches can be tightened by increasing the hoop size. Some trappers hoop beavers using metal hog rings rather than heavy thread or cord. Leg holes should be trimmed and sewn or nailed closed. These are not the rules of the sonnet.

FLESHING SKUNK

Skin as described for the raccoon or mink. Flesh all flesh and fat from the leather on a fleshing beam or board. When fleshed, soak the pelt in vinegar for one-half hour to remove most of the scent from both the pelt and your hands. Rinse, turn the fur out and hang loose by the nose in an airy place, until the fur side is dry. When dry, turn fur side in and place on a standard drying board or wire stretcher. Fasten with closely spaced nails around the skirt. Spread the tail open and nail that way. Use a belly board. Hang in a cool, dry place until dry. When dry, remove from the board and again store in a cool, dry place. Hang in a cool dry / when dry / till dry / store / in a cool dry place.

PROVENANCE

Born in Providence, she was a lifelong Providence resident
Born in Providence, he had lived in Cumberland for 52 years
Born in Cranston, she had lived in Cranston until 1964
Born in Boston, she had lived in Providence for 32 years
Born in Providence, he was a lifelong resident of Providence
Born in Providence, she had lived in Seekonk most of her life
Born in the Azores, he had lived in Fall River most of his life
Born in Fall River, he had lived in Fall River for many years
Born in Cape Verde, she had lived in Providence for 43 years
Born in Providence, he had lived in Cranston since 1956
Born in North Attleboro, she lived in Attleboro all her life
Born in South Attleboro, he had lived in Pawtucket most of his life
Born in Pawtucket, he was a lifelong resident of Pawtucket
Born in Quebec, he had lived in Pawtucket since 1914
Born in India, he came to this country in 1989
She was a direct descendant of a passenger on the Mayflower
Born in Providence and a lifelong resident of the city
Born in Providence, she had lived in Providence for many years
Born in Providence, he had lived in Providence before moving to California in 1954
Born in Barrington, she had lived in Barrington for 77 years, and in Warwick for 10
Born in West Warwick, she had lived in Coventry most of her life
Born in Warren, she had lived in North Providence since 1939
Born in Smithfield, she was a lifelong resident of the town

OF

She was a daughter of
She was the sister of the late
He was the companion of
He was the husband of the late
He was the father of
He was the father of the late
And brother of the late
She was the mother of the late
She was the sister of the late
He was the husband of

PASTIMES

She enjoyed crocheting & gardening
He enjoyed painting & drawing
She enjoyed reading
She enjoyed riding her Harley-Davidson
She was an avid bingo player
She enjoyed knitting, crocheting and reading
She enjoyed reading
She was a member of the former Jayceettes

WORK

A retired weaver:
He had worked as a lace weaver at various mills in Pawtuxet Valley
for more than 40 years.
A retired textile worker:
She had been a braider-tender at the former Providence Braid Co.
for 35 years.
A head wire inspector:
She had been head inspector of quality control at the former United Wire Co.
for over 40 years.
A retired assembler:
She had been an assembler at the former General Electric base plant
in Providence.
A retired hospital employee:
He had worked in the laundry and kitchen at Cushing Hospital for 20 years.
A retired nurse supervisor:
She cared for handicapped adults and children.
A retired textile worker:
She had worked at the King Phillip-Berkshire Mill for over 40 years.
A former store department manager:
She had been employed in the leather goods department for 30 years.
A retired major with 27 years of service:
She served on the Island of Saipan in the Mariannes Islands with an
advance medical group during World War II.
A retired fabric cutter:
He had been a cutter at the former Pilgrim Cutter Company.

ANOTHER OLD MAN OF BARCELONA

On the afternoon of June 7, 1926, a distracted old man ... [was struck by a tram] ... [a]t the corner of Gran Via and Bailèn Street. The victim carried no identification in his jacket making it impossible to identify him. *The jacket, torn by the shock, caught the old man in its familiar sleeves and lining, hackles rising like sodden wooden grain, the weave here tight, panning like roof tiles, there loose, like magnified herringbone.* Though still breathing he was badly hurt and covered with blood. *Pumping like paint from squeezed tubes. Then lacy festoons like egg yolk descending. Then filmy crimson pulled like blinds over the white of an eye. Then translucent like the marbleized skein in which muscle is wrapped.* He lay on the ground next to the tracks *which raised themselves up on one elbow to look at him.* Mistaken for a beggar, the dying old man was transported by ambulance to Hospital de la Santa Creu, [where] ... [t]hree days [later] ... [he] died, in a small and empty room *the ceiling of which rolled back like the tide when he passed.*

LETTERS FROM JOE OLIVER

To his niece:

—Thank God I only need one thing & that is clothes.

—I get little money from an agent for the use of my name & after I pay room rent & eat I don't have much left.

To his sister from his boardinghouse at 508 Montgomery Street:

—I always feel like I've got a chance. I still feel I'm going to snap out of the rut I've been in for several years.

To his sister:

—I've started a little dime bank saving. Got $1.60 in it & I won't touch it. I am going to try to save myself a ticket to New York.

— I have helped to make some of the best names in the music game, but I am too much of a man to ask those that I have helped to help me.

—Should anything happen to me will you want my body?

—I may never see New York again in my life. Don't think I am afraid … I am trying to live near to the Lord than ever before. So I feel like the Good Lord will take care of me.

Monday, February 14, 2005

RE: MOVEMENT OF YOUR CONSIGNMENT

Dear Dr. Welies,

Thank you for your urgent message. This seems to be a case of mistaken identity. I am neither an honorable contractor nor a man.

You need not concern yourself that I will inform the Diplomatic Courier Services that the crate labeled "Diplomatic Documents" which you are sending from Nigeria to London via the United States on an Express Cargo Flight does not contain vital "Diplomatic Documents" as declared but actually "Money." I will not be contacting Mr. Edy Smithkline at the Global Trust Diplomatic Courier Services about this or any other matter as today I plan to focus my energies on selecting 10 good examples of pattern poetry to show my students next week.

There is therefore no need for you to come here for your 10% share.

Thank you for your kind blessing,

Sincerely,

Mairéad Byrne

PUTTENHAM'S FORMS FOR PATTERN POETRY

"The lozange called rhombus"
"The fuzie or spindle called romboides"
"The triangle, or triquet"
"The square or quadrangle"
"the pillaster or cillinder"
"The spire or taper, called piramis"
"The rondel or sphere"
"The egg or figure oual"
"The triquet reuerst"
"The triquet displayed"
"The taper reuerved"
"the rödel displayed"
"The lozange reuersed"
"The egge displayed"
"the lozange rabbated"

FOUND

At Battersea

undivided attention
& loyalty:

Catherine Boucher
X
William Blake

RED SKELETON INTERVIEWS NERVE ENDS, FILAMENTS, & AN ELECTROLYTE

RS   So guys …

NFE   **EEEEEEEEEEEEEEEEEEEEKKKKKKK!!!!!!!!!**

RS   Hey! That's quite a shriek. Seriously guys …

NFE   *ccchhhggggttttcchhhh* [*abrupt sound made by pushing air forcefully through cheek using reflex propulsive tongue action*]

RS   So you're doing the gig …

NFE   *nnnnncccchhhhgggggghhhhkk!!!!!!!!!!!*

RS   Huh-huh. Huh-huh. I see where you're going with this …

NFE   *EEEeee—EEeeugh—eugh—eugh—eugh—eugh* [*agonizing creaking/ back-of-throat grinding*]

RS   Yeah I see it!

NFE   *SSSKKKRREEEEEEEEEEEENNNNNKKKkkk-k-k-k* [*hideous chalkboard scraping*]

RS   I kinda see it …

RED SKELTON INTERVIEWS JOSEPH THE CARPENTER

Joseph, you were born …
—Woe to the day on which I was born into the world! Woe to the womb which bare me! Woe to the bowels which admitted me!

And you were raised by your …
—Woe to the breasts which suckled me! Woe to the feet upon which I sat and rested! Woe to the hands which carried me and reared me until I grew up!

I'm sure she did her best …
—For I was conceived in iniquity, and in sins did my mother desire me.

Well okay, let's talk about your education …
—Woe to my tongue and my lips, which have brought forth and spoken vanity, detraction, falsehood, ignorance, derision, idle tales, craft, and hypocrisy! Woe to mine eyes, which have looked upon scandalous things! Woe to mine ears, which have delighted in the words of slanderers! Woe to my hands, which have seized what did not of right belong to them!

But not your bowels …
—Woe to my belly and my bowels, which have lusted after food unlawful to be eaten! Woe to my throat, which like a fire has consumed all that it found!

Joseph, you have based yourself principally in Galilee, traveling a little in Judea and Samaria. Have you ever wished to travel more widely?
—Woe to my feet, which have too often walked in ways displeasing to God! Woe to my body; and woe to my miserable soul, which has already turned aside from God its Maker! What shall I do when I arrive

at that place where I must stand before the most righteous Judge, and when He shall call me to account for the works which I have heaped up in my youth?

I don't know Joseph. It's a problem for everyone ...
—Woe to every man dying in his sins!

That's a bit harsh ...
—Assuredly that same dreadful hour, which came upon my father Jacob, when his soul was flying forth from his body, is now, behold, near at hand for me.

Surely not!
—Oh! how wretched I am this day, and worthy of lamentation!

Well it's been nice having you on the program Joseph.
—But God alone is the disposer of my soul and body ...

And so from Red Skelton & Joseph the Carpenter to everyone listening ...
—He also will deal with them after His own good pleasure!

Goodnight & God bless!

AN INTERVIEW WITH A WISE OLD MAN

MB: You are a wise old man & have lived a long time. Please can you tell me what you have learned?

WOM: Yes.

MB: For example, you have built the house you live in. You use energy powered only from the natural movements of insects in your garden. You have perfected a mineral supplement which, in effect, replaces the necessity for food. You make all your own clothes out of cloth woven by yourself from flax grown in the far field yonder. You have had six wives, each one younger & more beautiful than the one before. All your children have emigrated but send you large packages. Everyone says you are incredibly wise. You have written many books. Today, in what may be the waning years of an incredibly productive life, you seem serene & equanimous. What is the secret of your happiness?

WOM: Happiness.

MB: I see. Very good. You often talk about "chalk," how things must be "chalky," and the essential "chalkiness" of experience. Can you expand on that?

WOM: I was a teacher.

MB: I know. I was your student. They say that everyone should have one great teacher in her. You were mine.

WOM: One feels one's students.

MB: That is so beautiful. You have received many honors in your life. You have won the Pulitzer Prize—twice, gotten four Guggenheims, a MacArthur "Genius" Award, and the Nobel—for both Peace & Literature. These achievements are like some aspiring writer's wet dream. What does it mean to have achieved so much?

WOM: I never got a Pushcart.

MB: Oh, I'm sorry. People say that true happiness is derived from living in the moment, that regardless of what has passed or passing or to come, the thing is to just be in the moment, as fully as possible. To smell the roses & coffee. To be aware of the small hairs rising on the forearm or the back of the neck, the cilia on the caterpillar, the smell of new-baked bread on the window-sill, the taste of a ripe mango, the sound of Bob Marley when his voice breaks or he makes one of those kinda sexual sounds. Is this what it's all about for you? Is this what has caused you to forge a path to wisdom?

WOM: Mm hmm.

MB: That's so great! I feel we're in sync which is weird because I'm not that wise even though I was your student all those years ago and am engaged to you now. But is it ever a strain for you—being a wise old man & having to go out & about wearing wise old man clothes & expressions? Do you ever wish you could just pig out or be unabashedly boorish & selfish like an ordinary old man & give the wisdom a miss for a while?

WOM: Yes.

MB: Oh come here you devil.

EXCERPT FROM AN INTERVIEW WITH CHARLES REZNIKOFF

MB: I read somewhere that you walk 18 miles every day around the city of New York. I read that when your wife, Marie Syrkin, invited you to come along on a trip to Israel you said you couldn't because you hadn't yet finished exploring Central Park. New York doesn't feature at surface level in your work but does its systematic grid, & your steady pacing of it, somehow permeate your work?

CR: I like walking.

MB: Poems are measured in feet; at least the metric foot was at one time the unit of measurement for the poetic line. Is there a sense in which your own poems are measured by the soles of your own feet, laid down again & again on the pavement of New York? On the sidewalks & streets? An invisible routine tracery on the sea-bed of the cacophonous city?

CR: I have my beaten tracks.

MB: Wallace Stevens was in the habit of walking to work at Hartford Accident & Indemnity. He must have been a character about town. People noticed him, & understood he was composing poetry on his walks. There's a story about someone observing Stevens suddenly walking backwards. "He's revising," the person said. Do you think your own composition is linked to the directionality of your stroll?

CR: My work has a type of carpet-bomb formation. I'm not sure it maps onto the pattern of two feet. Maybe some version is true, e.g., my work is to my feet as New York is to my feet but my work & New York are not at all alike nevertheless.

MB: That's kind of Aristotelian. Let's talk about hands. Do you know *There's the church / And there's the steeple / Open the doors / & there's the people*. Look you can see them wiggling …

TO MY SURPRISE I FIND MYSELF IN POSSESSION OF THE GLAMOROUS FACTS

The distance from New York City to Boston?
—Approximately 4 hours. By car.

The breeding cycle of periodic cicadas?
—Occurs at prime number intervals of 7, 13, and 17 years.

The "tiles" in the floor of the archway at the entrance to Trinity College, Dublin?
—Are of course blocks: Elizabethan, hexagonal, wooden, and reversible. To counter wear.

—Quiet. I know what it is. It is a human hand.

INTERVIEW

No comment.

No comment.

I would like to be able to comment on that but I know very little about anything except poetry.

No comment.

I know what fascia board is.

Just about.

No comment.

Yes.

Well no, you have me there.

Qatar.

I can talk about enjambment.

Yes.

SHORT INTERVIEW

Q. So what is it like to be not a prize-winner?

A. It's okay I guess. I mean, it's nothing special. Plenty of people don't win prizes.

Q. Come now you're being modest. *Get the photo, Ted.*

A DIALOGUE BETWEEN RON SILLIMAN & WILLIAM BLAKE

BLAKE: *!!!!THGIS YM FO TUO TEG*

HAPPINESS LEVELS 1994-2004

1994: 8
1995: 7
1996: 9
1997: 10
1998: 8
1999: 7
2000: 8
2001: 7
2002: 2
2003: 3
2004: 7

TODAY'S SELF-HATRED COUNTS

0000-0700: MEDIUM
0700-0900: LOW
0900-1100: HIGH
1100-1200: MEDIUM
1200-1300: LOW

Outlook: LOW TO MEDIUM LEVELS FOR REMAINDER OF DAY

THE 9TH SNEEZE

Bless you!
Bless you.
bless you
bless YOU!
blessyou
bless ym
blsm
bm

REVIEWING THE 20TH CENTURY

The age artists were when they made the work collected in this room of the museum:

27
27
27
28
29
29

32
32
32
34
34
34
34
34
34
35
36
36
36
37
38

42
43
45
45
46
46

51
52
52
53
54
56
57
58
58
59

Modal age of artists when they made the work collected in this room of the museum:

34

THE MIDDLE

I've got to the middle
Whew!
I'm middle-aged
Whew!
I didn't get killed
Whew!
I didn't kill myself
Whew!
I'm middle-income
Whew!
I'm middle-rank
Whew!
I'm alright
I'm OK
I'm acceptable
Whew!
Yay!

GREAT BUSINESS IDEAS #9: TEST-YOUR-POETRY

**VIGOROUS YOUNG COMPANY PLANTS CHALLENGING AUDIENCES
FOR YOU—*OR* YOUR ENEMIES!**

Test **YOUR** poetry on our dedicated audiences of

*NON-ENGLISH SPEAKERS!

*MEN SERVING TIME!

*CHILDREN!

*RICH PEOPLE!

*ENTIRE CLIENTELE OF YOUR LOCAL GYM!

We can arrange for your **VERY SMALL** homogeneous poetry
audience to be **REPLACED** by a much **LARGER** homogeneous
audience in any of our popular categories!

Audiences can also be clothed in **LIME GREEN, HAIRY WOOL,** or
NUDE, for additional ELECTRIFYING effect.

Imagine your rival's horror when confronted by a sea of
STEWARDESSES or **WRESTLERS** in thongs rather than the meager
bunch of poetry types expected!

You can test YOUR OWN POETRY too! Try out new material on
ACROBATS! On RECENT IMMIGRANTS! On THE TERMINALLY
ILL! For a special fee, we can even arrange for an audience of
your OWN FAMILY! Find out if your poetry relates to YOUR OWN FLESH
& BLOOD! NO COUSIN TOO DISTANT TO TRACK DOWN!!!
NO MOTHER TOO SURLY!!!

******SPECIAL******
For a limited time only YOUR reading or your ENEMY'S can be filmed
with WILD CLAPPING by UNIFORMED POLICE* or SENIORS** as
appropriate.

**Only these two groups available for wild clapping momentarily
but expansion plans are in the offing.* ** ditto

HE IN THE BIOS OF 21 IRAQI POETS

He he higher the where he he the where the He the he the He the published published

He the the He He

the he He the where the the published He He the He where he

He He the the the the he the He the he published He Shelley Hughes other He southern He the he teacher then He Teachers' the He "The other the he prophetic They where the"

He then he He then when he He when where he the He published published

He published He Rothenberg others He published the

He He the He teaches the

He the he He he then the He He published the

he the where he the He published the he the the the He the theme the he published th

he There he published he the where he he published published

He where he the the published He the the

He He He published published he

the the the

He the He published

She She She

He the He the where he published He

HASHEM He published then where he He published

he He he the he he *the* the the published

She Her published she published She

the He He The He published the the he he published published the

SHE IN THE BIOS OF 21 IRAQI POETS

published published

published
published **Shelley**

published published
published published

published
published published published published published
published
published published

published
She She She
published
HASHEM published published
published
She published **she** published **She**
published
published published

HE IN THE BIOS OF 21 IRAQI POETS EDITED

He he higher the where he he the where the He the he the He the published
published

He the the He He

    he He the he He the where hthe th He He the He where he

He He the the the the he the He the he published He Shelley Hughes other He
southern He the he teacher then He Teachers' the He "The other the he proph[...]
They where the"

He then he He then when he He when where he the He published published

He published He   He published the

He He the He teaches the

He the he He he then the He He published the

he the where he the He published the he the the He the theme the he publishe[...]

he There he published he the where he he published published

He where he the the published He the the

He He He published published he

the the the

He the He published

She She She

He the He the where he published He

HASHEM He published then where he He published

he He he the he he //te

She Her published she published She

the He He The He published the the he he published published

SHE IN THE BIOS OF 21 IRAQI POETS EDITED

publishe   she

published
published Shelley

published publishe
published publishe

publishe
published published published published publishe
publishe
published publishe

publishe
She She She
publishe
HASHEM published publishe
publishe
She publishe **she** publishe **She**
publishe

published publishe

THEY

The new 3rd person singular.

BAGHDAD

They come, we stop them and we pound them and they go and when we stop they return.
—Iraqi Minister of Information, Mohammed Saeed al-Sahaf, April 5, 2003

if I leave Baghdad early towards Baghdad will never reach Baghdad will never come to Baghdad are nowhere near Baghdad not near Baghdad **near Baghdad** armoured push towards Baghdad approached Baghdad push into Baghdad advance on Baghdad forces drove into Baghdad in the raid into Baghdad probing mission in Baghdad not even 100 miles from Baghdad 10 miles from central Baghdad just seven miles from Baghdad on the outskirts of Baghdad to make it into Baghdad home to Baghdad fly on into Baghdad home free to Baghdad little more than one hour from Baghdad an hour and a half short of Baghdad encirclement of Baghdad siege of Baghdad to choke Baghdad cut Baghdad in half so to speak pulled back to Baghdad back to Baghdad highway to Baghdad main road going into Baghdad main road going into Baghdad to Baghdad on Baghdad to Baghdad over Baghdad fleeing Baghdad sky over parts of Baghdad on what parts of Baghdad vast areas of Baghdad south-east of Baghdad into southern Baghdad Baghdad's southern Baghdad from the east south-western areas of Baghdad beyond northwest of Baghdad from southern Baghdad They're in Baghdad actually in the city of Baghdad inside Baghdad in central Baghdad in the heart of Baghdad in the heart of Baghdad penetrate the heart of Baghdad into the centre of Baghdad to smash rocked the centre of Baghdad stacked up over Baghdad enveloping Baghdad penetrating Baghdad isolated Baghdad swept low over Baghdad thrust into Baghdad night-time bombing of Baghdad the people of Baghdad had the poor of Baghdad the people of Baghdad deserted streets of western Baghdad in the streets of Baghdad on a house in Baghdad's **street dogs of Baghdad** convoy out of Baghdad Battle of Baghdad All across Baghdad vast areas of Baghdad vast areas of Baghdad vast, flat city of Baghdad Baghdad's hospitals liberated Baghdad *Hi you guys. I'm in Baghdad* outside Baghdad inside Baghdad Baghdad burning 18 blue and black arrows around Baghdad fell on Baghdad head out of Baghdad Leaving Baghdad history of Baghdad As we left Baghdad

TRAPPED

house is trashed. near the ruined market. thick crust of sand.
render non-existent whole buildings by remote control. destroying
all six houses. breaking nearly every window on the street. demolishing
burning ramshackle auto repair shop. gutting small diner. destroying.
burn to death inside their car. school damaged   bombs detonated above
a residential home.   school. tearing apart top floor. shrapnel. and breaking
most of school's windows. strewn with wreckage. bloodstains on a
sidewalk. blood-soaked children's slippers. water
seeping   ruptured pipes. corrugated iron   said
dangling
from roofs of damaged shops. " " umbilical wires and
broken concrete. trapped under   rubble.
screamed demolished office and several nearby
houses. said
turned block " " into rubble rubble from the smashed
and smoldering hit rattling windows of a gaping gash slammed
into homes and shops buildings into charnel houses. twisted metal.
rubble everywhere. rest is ashes.

RUBBLE

dug through **rubble** frantically **rubble** strewn over marble split open like dolls' houses
cut down inside living room brick hut single-storey corrugated iron and cement
two-room brick right through windows walls shaking building shake
bombed
house.   hundreds of small holes in the walls of the upstairs
roof patio.
broken glass at the
entrance, we entered _____
in Baghdad.   rooms are   disarray. Several walls cracked,
windows all shattered and a thick layer of dust/grime
exposed furniture, books, carpets and floors.
windows shattered and the
doors were blown out.
rubble
hospital destroyed bombs missing in **rubble** were
buried this morning crumpled
crushed windows of sixteen all broken crouching in **rubble**
gaping windows and wrecked houses windows blew
in
blows out all the glass from the windows damage
to windows **rubble**
from walls large blood stained mattress on floor
crushed in **rubble** of farmhouse
pulverized by missiles with
built of soft brown stone, and the explosion
house's outer walls like butter
small crater and pockmarks of shrapnel damage scattered across house walls
grey-powdered **rubble**

BROKEN

I've seen wars in former Yugoslavia and Africa and I know that what it takes a few seconds to take apart—buildings, communities, lives—will take years to put together again, if they ever can be. —Alex Renton, Oxfam International

Swayed like treehouse   how Zaid

   or Asmaa

       and Israa

           and Mimi

                  and Omar

       or Majid

        and Raid or Ibrahim

   or Umal
 or Waleed
or Samir

    or Hamsa **said** houses

        and small shops

burning

       ramshackle auto

       repair   top floor

               with shrapnel   and breaking

               most of

    shop gutting

         small diner

   school damaged   picture bodies
                      two children

bombs tearing   exposed bones
                     intestines

   It's funny   demolished
watching things
being broken

  turned block into rubble   smashed and smoldering

                      " "

               " "

    " "   " "

"   " "   " "

                " "   " "

METAPHOR, SIMILES

like grapes from the sky

like small grapefruit

metal butterflies

like small stones

like cough sweets in a metal sheath

like a treehouse

like dolls' houses

like butter

like a bell with a very hollow ring

like a doll in a funeral shroud

like heavy wooden furniture being moved in an empty room

AN ALMOST WELCOME SPLASH OF COLOR

large blood stained mattress on floor
Three spots of blood from dead people
daughters lying in their own blood near the door
blood spurting from their boots
blood of two sheep
bloodstains on a sidewalk.
blood-soaked children's slippers

ALMOST

Suicide Bomber Almost Kills 50 at Police Station in Iraq (REUTERS)
Guerrilla Raid in Restive Iraq Town Leaves 22 Almost Dead (REUTERS)
Moscow Pool Roof Collapse Almost Kills 26, Search Goes On (REUTERS)
China Shopping Mall Fire Almost Kills at Least 53 (REUTERS)
U.S. Soldier Almost Dies, Five Held in Iraq Council Killing (REUTERS)
Four U.S. Troops Wounded, Iraqi Almost Killed in Ambush (REUTERS)
Palestinian Suicide Bomber Almost Kills 8 in Jerusalem (REUTERS)
Rumsfeld Assesses Iraq Security; Bomb Almost Kills 13 (REUTERS)
Nearly 600 Almost Killed in Powerful Morocco Quake (REUTERS)
Iraq Leaders Call for Calm After Attacks Almost Kill 165 (REUTERS)
More Than 20 Almost Killed in Attacks on Pakistan Shi'ites (REUTERS)
Six Palestinians Almost Die in Failed Attack on Israelis (REUTERS)
Baltimore Water-Taxi Capsizes, 2 Almost Dead, 3 Missing (REUTERS)
Six Almost Killed in Anti-Aristide March in Haiti (REUTERS)

UNOPENED EMAIL

BREAKING: New Torture Photos Released

HEADLINES

TINY ORGASM POPS OVER BAGHDAD
PERSONS RISK GENTLENESS
WOMAN BRINGS MAN TO BRINK AS MISSILES LAUNCH
NO SEX SAYS PRESIDENT SINCE 1993
TROOPS SEEK PRIVACY TO HANDLE COCKS
STRANDED BODY PARTS WEEP
BRIT SEMEN SPARKS DESERT FLOWER
PILOT NAVIGATES BY VAGINAL ACHE
FINGER SLIPS INTO INTIMATE ZONE
CITY RUMMAGED FOR GUERILLA KISS

CHOOSE YOUR HUSBAND

War Activist: *You should be shot in the head*
Peace Activist: *No. You should be shot in the head*

FACING THE MUSIC

It's not frost: it's snow
It's not backfire: it's gun-fire
It's not fun: it's alcoholism
It's not a tantrum: it's violence
It's not witty: it's abuse
It's not marriage: it's divorce
It's not anger: it's rage
It's not nothing: it's a lump
It's not fear: it's reality
It's not sleep: it's death
It's not *au revoir*: it's the end

CROP

I THOUGHTXXXXXXXXXXXXXXXXX
XXXXXXBECAUSE YOU SAW ME
XXXXXXXXSLICED &XXXXXXXXX
XXXXXXXXXXXTORN OPENXXXXXX
XXXXXXXXXXXX&XXXXXXXXXXXX
XXXXXTHE SHINING CHILDXXXXX
XXXXXXXXXXDRAGGED FROM ME
XXXXXXYOU WOULD HAVEXXXXX
XXXSTAYED WITH USXXXXXXXXX
XXXXXXXXXXFOR LIFEXXXXXXXX
XXXXXXXXXXXXXXXXXXXXXXXXXX
XXXXXXXXXBUT NOT SOXXXXXXX

TEDIUM

I park the green car in the rain and go in the red door to collect my child:
My child whose face is a white petal detaching and fluttering toward me.
I park the green car under the clouds and go in the red door for my child:
My child whose dark hair falls over her head as she bends to her drawing.
I park the green car in the tight sun and go in the red door to collect my child:
My child deep in a cluster of children sticking colored paper to paper:
My child who shouts out: *Can I finish this first?* I am thinking about divorce.
I park the green car in the sun and go in the red door to collect my child:
My child who hurtles toward me/I swing her around/then Yang-Yang hurtles towards me/
I swing Yang-Yang around/Her father is coming in nine days to take her.
I park the green car in the rain and go in the red door for my child:
My child who stands by the wall in the gymnasium with other wallflowers hanging her head.
I park the green car in the rain and go in the red door for my child:
My child pounding the floor of the gymnasium with her strong little calves.
I park the green car in the sun and go in the red door for my child:
My child who is not in the cafeteria/and not in the gymnasium/and not in the first playground
But there—in the kindergarten playground on the slide—upside down is my child.
I park the green car in the sky and go in the red door for my child:
My child whose face is a white petal detaching and fluttering towards me.

REMINISCENCE

Everything was perfect about our relationship except the speed with which names changed.

He had wonderful smooth muscles and one day I would say *You have such wonderful muscles* and he would preen. But next day, when I would praise him again, he would laugh *You silly, those aren't muscles—they are roubaloos!*

Then, on Wednesday, I might say *I love your roubaloos* and he would say *What are you talking about, they're blapdocks ...*

And pretty soon he was interrupting me: *Don't speak! I have told you a million times these are estrudels. And they're mine!*

Well, you have beautiful hair, I said. *You little ninny—that's not hair, that's persillis.* And so it would go.

He'd punch his finger in my shoulder and say: *How difficult can it be to remember a name?*

THE WAY OF THE WORLD

The soldier met the woman half-way.
"You killed my daughter," she said.
"Yeah, I'm sorry about that," the soldier replied.
"But do you remember when I asked you for water
you refused me—
you wouldn't treat a dog like that.
So I'm sorry about your daughter—
I hope you're sorry about the water too."
"It's not the same thing," said the woman.
"Not to you maybe," said the soldier.
"But who can account for how another person feels?
"You raped and killed my daughter," said the woman.
"I didn't rape her. We had consensual sex."
"She was six."
"Look, there are mistakes on both sides.
We both have to live with that.
Your daughter is gone, get over it.
What I could use from you right now is water."

THIS IS NOT ARLINGTON

Though the sky is cobalt & grey & mauve. Though the leaves are heavy with green & rain. Though the grass is crew-cut & militant.

Picture a park. Or part of a park. A lawn, vista, or stretch.

Strewn across the cropped green, the yellow-tinged tufts—*wallets!* Men's wallets. Mostly black. Shiny & supple. Soft from pockets, chests, palms, hips, thighs. Plumpish, slightly rounded.

All are flipped open. Displaying photos of children. School photos. Two by threes and "wallets." Emptied of everything. Except children. Gap-toothed. Nervous. Grinning. Glum. Sheepish. Wry. Exultant. Scared. Disproportionate. Perky. Covering their teeth.

Hundreds, thousands of children. All shades. Multitudinous as raindrops. Flung across the grass.

Farther than the eye can see.

A LOVING AUDIENCE IS NECESSARY

and then oh my god and then suddenly jeepers I nearly
what do you think but what should I what should we
do you think we you won't believe I was oh my god
you know how well it was like that remember that
was anyway it was like when remember when
do you think we what if we don't
do you will you really it was scary oh my god
you know how well you know how so
look at you there I was you can imagine well
guess what hey baby hey my sweetheart what
about you though will you be do you think we
will we be it's a with you us us
we could we may do you think we let's let's what
do you think should we or we might oh my god
you know how well it was like
that it was crazy you know how

AN EDUCATED HEART

El cora-zon-ed-u-cado
Huay   de shing
↑   schuay ↓ ↑
     ↓
Hway shoo-eh deh sheeng
Gyo yook eui mah eum
Kyeogh yuke oo-eh mah-um
Oon Cŏ–rah-sŏn Ehh–doo–că–dŏ
Croí foghlamtha
Croí eolasach
Croí oilte
Croí feasach
Ein gebildetes hertz
Hertzenbildung
Un coeur savant
Un ker savan
Oon cohdahsohn e-thoo-kah-thoh
Oon cor-ath-sone eh-doo-ca-dho
Meu coraçăo educādo
Mih cora-sew ee-duc-ad-oo
Hui Xin
Huay shing
Kyōyōnoaru kokoro

LARCENY

In black dress
I break
into marriage
twice

Once for a fair child
Once for a dark

DEFINITION OF SNUG

head
wedged between
shoulder &
head

cheek against shoulder

elbow on belly
fist under chin

fingers curled
around leg

thigh under legs
calf over calf

feet
folded in

wings

HAPPINESS

Five steps between my room & yours.
The two of us here.

OUR COLDS

could be flu
cat allergies
or carbon monoxide poisoning

but probably not
all three

SHOULD BE & IS

The car should be in the driveway
& it is
The girls should be asleep in their rooms
& they are
One Two
The heat should come on in a minute
& it does
The water should get hot after running
& it does
The keys should be in my coat pocket
& they are
The door should be locked when I lock it
& it is

FRIDAY NIGHT

I'm a miserable person:
What have I in life
but my two daughters,
wine,
& poetry?

PRIVACY

If you do not have a room
body odor can be a room.

What then is a house?

OPEN HOUSE

Come into my house.
I do not want it anymore.

A MAN COMES TO THE HOUSE

A man comes to the house.
It is the plumber.
He tells me about caulking
& says
You do not have a sink.
You have a bowl.

A man comes to the house.
It is the furnace man.
There is something inevitable about him.

A man comes to the house.
This man can do everything.
He is Italian
& has wild red hair.

A man comes to the house.
It is another plumber & his helper.
They put in a new water heater
& take the old one away.
Then plug the cracks in the furnace
with furnace cement.

A man comes to the house.
He is a mason.
Everything crumbles, he says.
And I say, *Not poetry.*

SOMETHING UNBELIEVABLE HAPPENED YESTERDAY

I fixed the leak!

BLISTERING COMPETENCE

I think I know how to use cotton buds in my ear thank you very much
I think I know how to boil water for 2 mins 40 secs before making tea thank you
I think I know how to pull up the handbrake while simultaneously releasing
    the trunk & opening the door with my chin thank you very much
I think I know how to dismantle the 9-year-old VCR to liberate the Martin Luther
    King videotape thank-you-VERY-much
I think I know how to change a furnace filter thank you *MUCH* obliged
I think I know how to drain the boiler and top up after the automatic feeder
    kicks in thank you for your concern no really
I think I know how to joke with a code monkey thank YOU!
I think I'm doing JUST FINE but *THANK YA!*

FIELD TRIP

On the yellow bus with the children—
in their seat belts of shout.

THAT OLD CHESTNUT ABOUT WHETHER TO SAVE THE BABY OR THE PAINTING FROM THE BURNING BUILDING

Silver tears
rained
from Charlene's eyes

sending me
dashing to the bus
for a lost glove

losing my notebook
with a month's work

answering that question
for myself after:

Would you give your full notebook
for a found glove

with

Gladly! Gladly!

No thrill greater than the finding of it
on the floor beneath the very last seat

except the triumph of my *I Found It* march maybe
& the open hand of Charlene
& Charlene's eyes & smile.

Poetry, my beloved secondary,
steps back for poetry.

# of course

of course
> my father brought home books to us every Saturday

of course
> they were second-hand

of course
> he had 8 children to think about

of course
> he brought us to art classes in the National Art Gallery

of course
> he brought us to the Young Scientists Exhibition

of course
> he brought us to the country & all the castles & ruins & forts

of course
> he brought us to the Phoenix Park & parked in the grass
> & held the door open & said *Out!*

of course
> he brought us to Dollymount Strand every Christmas morning

of course
> he made trifle

of course
> he made "wafers"

of course
> he bought small bars of chocolate & divided them in 8

of course
> he divided up the heels of sliced pans & sliced loaves
> & made us all eat a piece

of course
> he mended our schoolbags

of course
> he built bookshelves

of course
> he loaded the groceries into the cupboard

of course
> he made lists

of course

he kept a file on each one of us with all our school reports

of course

he took me to the theatre

of course

I danced around so much under my small umbrella that he told my mother he would never take me out again

of course

he took my sisters with him on trips to weather stations in remote parts of the country

of course

he loved Irish

of course

he went to his own church

of course

he walked home for lunch every day, with the *Irish Times* under his arm

of course

he never really knew his parents

of course

his father rejected him

of course

he was an intellectual without any pretensions

of course

I teased him & called him *Baldy*

of course

he brought us *Spangles* from the North

of course

he called from the phone-box down the street & said he was in Malin Head

of course

he came strolling in 10 minutes later & we all laughed our heads off

of course

life stopped when the knock came to the door & we were told that he had drowned

THE SKY

God's television.

ON WALKING PAST THE USS MIDWAY

The world is a lot bigger than poetry.
Not my world though.

ONE DROP

If it looks like a poem, it is a poem.
If it associates with poems, it is a poem.
If it has even one drop of poetry, it is a poem.
If it joins with another genre to form a new genre that genre will be poetry
& all its products will be poems.

DONALD HALL WOULD HATE ME

if he knew me
I don't want to be great

it takes me 10 minutes
to write a poem

sometimes
& then

I want to whisper or
shout it about
town

My poems are *usually brief*
they *resemble each other*
they *are anecdotal*
they *do not extend themselves*
they *make no great claims*
they *connect small things to other small things*

I LIKE SHORT!

I just want to kick the leaves
& have done

OBVIOUSLY

I have to get out of the tub:
I don't have
Internet access in here.

I'M FINE, I CAN WRITE

I have a cold & I'm in a work frenzy but
I'm fine, I can write.

I have that thing with my yoke & that yoke with my thing but
I'm fine, I can write.

I'm sobbing like Ben Stiller walking on his own solid legs away from Mary
but I'm fine, I can write.

I'm broke. It's so long since I've seen money I refer to it as *fluid assets*.
But I'm fine, I can write.

My hair seems to be falling out & my eye-lids look like scrotal sacs
but I'm fine, I can write.

Oops! Here's death, *hey*
I'm fine, I can write.

HOLIDAYS

The Muse came back from her holidays.
Wearily I got out of bed.
It was 5.24am.
I didn't know Muses took holidays.
Just get your pen, she said.

DECIPHERING MY HAND

Aslan Banking
Ashen Building
Altan Brisbane
Asher Brisket
Allen Ginsberg

CONCEPT

Whitman was economical.

SCARY CONCEPT

I am profligate.

STEPS TO THE INVISIBLE POETRY FESTIVAL

bus
bus
train
plane
bus
bus
cab

MAKING THE POETRY FESTIVAL VISIBLE

RIPTA
Bonanza
Silver Line
Aer Lingus
Bus Éireann
Bus Éireann
Douglas Street Cabs

THE STIGMA OF SELF-PUBLICATION

I am *so* over it.

PLANNING THE POETRY READING

A poem about childbirth.
A poem about savings.
An interesting movie idea.
A poem about silence.
A poem about the Rhode Island State House.
A poem about Baghdad.
A poem about clarity.
A poem about glorious routine.
A poem about time.
A poem about planning.
Another poem about planning.
A poem about emigration.
A poem about poverty.
A poem about being a single parent.
A poem about metaphor.
A poem about Louis Armstrong.
A poem about *The Wind That Shakes the Barley*.
A poem about a scrubbie.

APPLAUSE

THANK-GOD-HE'S-DONE
THANK-GOD-HE'S-DONE
THANK-GOD-HE'S-DONE
THANK-GOD-HE'S-DONE
THANK-GOD-HE'S-DONE
THANK-GOD-HE'S-DONE

AUDIENCE

ON THE WAY TO THE STAGE IN *THE SMELL*

Last night I read in the *The Smell* in LA. It was tremendously exciting. Think about it. *The Smell in LA!* We drank beer from the neck in the bar next door which was exactly like a pub on the quays in Dublin except for the guys in white 10 gallon hats studded along the bar. Then Ara & Stan collected us. We were hustled to the stage door. Chains rattled. Padlocks swung. Not really but that's what it felt like. Guys looking like lookouts looked out. The battered steel door eased open. We filed through. It was like entering a container tank. Inside was a dark alley with black walls hung with lurid paintings. We could see the wings up ahead, the bright stage. We sloped through backstage. It was unbearably cool. We had our people. They had their people. All we lacked was instrument cases. Then suddenly we stopped. Turned round. It was like a sock. Cutting the cord. The original cul-de-sac. Their guys dragged broken car seats from alongside the walls. We were rooted to our spot. I noticed a slanting mike. Behind that—a pile of black. Behind that—the entrance, now the exit, through which we had come. The roadies (poets) pushed the carseats into 4 or 5 rows. The audience (poets) sat down. The emcee (poet) got the show on the road. The (poets) read, our poems suspended in the trampoline throb of someone's else's music on a stage we never reached.

POETRY

The perfect art form for those who like to avoid crowds.

how long does it take to write a poem?

time stands still

ON CHALKSTONE IN SPRING

Someone lifted up
the very big bowl
of sky
complete with
contrails
purple clouds
& scorched
blues

& didn't
quite
set it down
again
letting some
weird atmosphere
& juiced song
leak

into these tiny
streets
even the most
ordinary of
which is slung
under cherry blossom
like quick flame beneath
cupped hands.

RAINBOW

nice white kids
clean up green margins
in black neighborhoods

saturday morning on chalkstone
yellow bus grimy already
black

children's faces
staring through windows
like moons,

sponges,
eager to soak up a joy
barely there—

cherry blossoms for a week in spring
gold drenchings of leaves—
flames—in October

always the incandescent sky
whose color
cannot be named

on the bridges, overpasses
republicans & democrats—
scraps—

peer through the wire
holding up paper signs—
every 10th car honks

maybe & every once in a while
the long rolling trumpet
of a truck

MOUNT PLEASANT

My dirty little Paris!
My funky neighborhood!
My busy bee!
My pavement crack walker!
My show-off!
My misery!
My scruffy Chalkstone!
My teetering Academy!
My *Poblanita*!
My *La Belle Boutique*!
My diesel fume webs!
My honkers!
My bashed cars!
My *Walgreens*!
My *Thai Star!*
My Hmong soccer team!
My confused sunflower!
My treasure trove!
My abandoned vehicle!
My *Dunkin Donuts!*
My Bakery *El Quiché*!
My *Print-It Plus!*
My *Pretty B Fashions!*
My closed broken-glass Castle Cinema!
My *Bajo Nueva Administracíon!*
My *Acme!*
My *Rincon Salvadoreño*!
My *Bolivian Restaurant!*
My *Family Dollar!*
My *Scrub-A-Dub!*

My *Pranzi!*
My *Tiende Y Panadeira Guatemalteca*
My *Vene* Mini Market!
My *Apt for Rent*
My *Pay by the Week*
My *Sale Pending!*
My Shell Station!
My *Shave Beard & Trim!*
My *Closed!*
My *Please Call Again!*
My Funeral Home!
My *All Kind Phone Card and Magazine*
My Tommy's Pizza!
My *Free Delivery!*
My *Under New Management!*
My eggplant pie!

I FIND A KNIFE

on river ave
cars jolt & play
the blade

triangular
without a haft

thinking of kids
I pick it up

& shield—or hide—
it with my
puffy envelope

& scour the streets
lathered with trash
for trash cans

till in the Professional
Building lot—
a dumpster

I lift the rubber flap
& think:
what if the trash is bagged?

the trash is bagged—
the closest bag is white

I sink the blade
up to its missing haft

so yes it's sharp

& I'm the guilty one

thinking of prints
a blade being flung

wanting to wipe my hand
of blood or rust or *what is that stuff*

but there's no part
of me

I'll let it touch

FEAR OF AIDS

I swallowed a child's tears.

GESTURE

A bundled up woman takes a bundled up child by the hand.

A woman bundled up in black holds a child bundled up in colors by the hand. They walk along Smith Street.

A woman in tight jeans walks away from me. She is holding the hand of a child in knitted cap & snow boots.

It is snowing. The children walk underneath the snow holding their mothers' hands.

It is Monday, December 4th, the first day of snow. The children are bundled up. Each child walks to school with their mother, holding her hand.

signs of love, smith street

he smiles up at her, way up
she tilts toward him

he pulls his back-pack on wheels,
manfully

she lifts his back-pack onto his back—
a very large postage stamp on a very small letter

she pats his back-pack
she pats its handle down

they walk
his small hand rises, like a lever, into hers

A POEM

a slim father
carries a small
child
&
a little girl
in a green coat
walks by
his left side
&
a taller boy
on his right
&
they wash
slightly from him

the girl
&
the boy
toward the
torn
chicken-wire fence
&   the
tangled grass
&
he
stepping back slightly
re-
leasing them
&
they   moving forward slightly
de-
taching from him
& then
each
letting go the
other

then the space
in between
& the children
gather speed   tumbling
toward school

the father
standing   watching

then lifting
the baby closer
picking up their morning

he turns

girl

on a side-street
late for school
stepping up
on a short wall
to sway
a few steps
alone

what it's possible to capture in words but not w/ a camera

on a stoop
in smith street
a girl &
a boy
so young
he's almost
another girl—
babies—
then his arms
drape her shoulders
then his left hand
suddenly
deep
inside his
checked
shorts

intersection

the red light
holds steady
while the plane
—miles above—
makes its incision
in the sky

on benefit street

theft:

of a white
geranium—
leaf &
blossom.

theft:

of a white
lilac—
leaf & blossom

exchange:

of a glance &
smile

EXCHANGE

I will tell you
something worth knowing
about immigration

If you will tell me
something worth knowing
about race

BLACK MAN STROLLING DOWN HILL MEETS WHITE WOMAN HUFFING UP: STRANGERS

BM: *Hi!* [I am not going to rob you]
WW: *Hi!* [Such a racist thought never entered my head]

ACRES OF COURTESY I WAS PREVIOUSLY UNAWARE OF

[regal wave]: *Be my guest*

[exposed palm, fingers spread]: *Thank you*

[exposed palm, fingers relaxed]: *You're welcome*

[brusque wave]: *Go now minion*

[body of car executing sinuous S-maneuver to allow other driver to cut through backed-up traffic to make a turn, beatific smiles]: *For this millisecond I am your true love forever*

PARKING IN FRONT OF SOMEONE ELSE'S HOUSE

After a while it feels like home.

COUPLE

against a tree
in the park

drinking
each other

I remember
that drink

UNDER THE TREES

trying to be more like the trees

—their great cat's head of sound

streaming from under the wind

—quitting trying—

then being more like the trees

CONTEMPORARY BELLS

My church broke out into a bit of contemporary bell ringing this morning.

The bells sort of made a frame for themselves & rolled around in it like skittles.

It was sort of trapezoid, with bumping sounds. The bells never gaining enough ground for melody but not losing hope of it either.

It was sort of maddening.

This happened at an odd time of the morning. Like 7.37 or 6.51.
Tactful bell-ringer perhaps. But there was no question of telling time.

The church is not my church exactly. Not in the sense that I go to it.
But I am aware of it. And have appreciated its bells.

FOR THE DRUM MAJOR

Who tried to give his life serving others
Who tried to love somebody
Who tried to be right on the war question
Who did try to feed the hungry
Who did try in his life to clothe those who were naked
Who did try in his life to visit those who were in prison
Who tried to love & serve humanity
Who was a drum major
Who was a drum major for justice
Who was a drum major for peace
Who was a drum major for righteousness
Who had no money to leave behind
Who had no fine & luxurious things of life to leave behind
Who just wanted to leave a committed life behind
And that's all

TO A MAN WITH STEEL LEGS

Picking your way elegantly across Smith Street
you are the epitome of poise.

If you are smaller than you once were
may you be taller as confidence grows?

Either way you're looking fine
in shorts.

TO A HILLY KIND OF CLIMBING FRAME

Meet my hands!
Meet my feet!
Meet my whole body draped
against yours—
undulant monkey bars!

TO A RACK OF CLOUDS

Yo clouds!
You got it right this time—
marching in peppy humps
across the horizon.

TO THE BOY AT THE CHECKOUT

if you could braid water
it might feel like this

cool chunks of air
a girl's hair

loading
the aisles

this store an ice-cube
& through its thick panes
the day

unbuckling

TO A MAN IN A BUTTERCUP SHIRT

Sunday evening
you stood quietly without attitude
on Bath, attentive,
your face drinking sun
your hands behind you
as if you just held them there
& you were not cuffed
while one cop probed with his fingers
the backseat
& the other turning you
& with the tips of his fingers
on your chest
pushed you
against the back
of your black car

TO A YOUNG MAN WHO HANGED HIMSELF
IN PROSPECT PARK

I think of you when I pass.
How you tended to yourself
that night
so you wouldn't be here
today.

TO A VERY SMALL JOGGER

What are you
emerging from dusk
but denser dusk
skipping—
assemblage of delight
down the boulevard

TO AN EAR LOBE

Relax
tender lobe
designed to be held
gently between finger & thumb—
perfect body part—
you are the reason for earrings
whose beauty too often
occludes yours

email me

for kari edwards

a voice is stilled
no more cantering small alphabets
skidding to listservs

no more of the fret & the tug of it,
the cold bit on the soft
warm tongue

just the trim syllables rising—in print
& on screen

enunciating what it is to write
what it is to be alive

TRUE EXCUSE

for Dugan

I cannot go to your memorial service.
I have to go to the circus that day.
But I remember you.

awake

to see
unwelcome date
george carlin
d. 6/22/08

NEGLECT

I think it's accurate to say this writer was neglected.
Someone neglected to tell him his crime.
He was left waiting a very long time.
Meanwhile the Germans laid siege to the city.
The food ran out.
Everyone spent all of their time running after it.
In prison there was nowhere to run
& no-one ever came
to feed him.
So he died.

DEATH OF A THOUGHTFUL & SERIOUS ANARCHIST

—Brad Will, in Oaxaca, October 27th 2006, aged 36

William Bradley Roland, aka Brad Will,
U.S. JOURNALIST/CAMERMAN, KILLED
Een reporter voor Indymedia New York,
WILLIAM BRADLEY ROLAND
In Santa Lucia del Camino
Hij voelde zich betrokken
More on **William Bradley Roland**
KILLED BY OAXACA PARAMILITARIES
a US journalist and camerman
shot and killed
aka Brad Will

WILLIAM BRADLEY ROLAND
US Journalist/Cameraman, Killed
a documentary filmmaker
ook gekend als Brad Will,
William Bradley Roland, aka Brad Will,
New York-based independent journalist
shot in the chest and killed,
by paramiliaries affiliated
Een reporter voor Indymedia New York
William Bradley Roland,
ook gekend als Brad Will

More on **William Bradley Roland**
a US journalist and camerman
shot and killed

I CANNOT MENTION HIS NAME

this cross between Don Corleone & Donald Duck
who quacked *Now I have the time to become a poet*

because if I were to mention his name
I would have to have

*clarity, knowledge, conviction, perspective, acuity,
searing vision, & bitter understanding*

none of which I have, about this particular customer,
hanged & taunted on the first day of Eid.

LIVE LINES

A cordon of his own words for Darrell Grayson, walking

"Mourning
Publicly, the tenderness in our hearts grows as the
Deadly hour draws near ..."
7/26/07 5:29PM
<u>0 comments</u>

"Can anyone convince anyone of the need to
Request heaven it open and saturate these
Dreams ...?"
7/26/07 5:31PM
<u>0 comments</u>

"From your patch of shade, bear witness
To those things seen looking side ways at the
Sun."
7/26/07 5:32PM
<u>0 comments</u>

"Viewed from a human point of view, what protection is there?"
7/26/07 5:34PM
<u>0 comments</u>

"Choice of life or death is contemplated.
A terrified beast of dubious lineage scurries to
and fro in concrete and steel geometrics."
7/26/07 5:35PM
<u>0 comments</u>

"In the batter of desperation, we seek council in the
tossing of bird legs ..."
7/26/07 5:35PM
0 comments

"We have come, as conscientious objectors, filing our appeals"
7/26/07 5:36PM
0 comments

"Mourning
Publicly, the tenderness in our hearts grows as the
Deadly hour draws near ..."
7/26/07 5:37PM
0 comments

"As the handful of sympathizers gathers for the execution vigil,
A pristinely clothed bird falls out of the waning sun,
On its back, into a bowl of gun-metal colored light
Before righting itself, on elegant red legs the mourning
Dove stands, its pink nails piercing the eye of the
Supreme Court building."
7/26/07 5:38PM
0 comments

"To them, vicarious sorrow
Is an alien, crushed on the shadow of a granite monument ..."
7/26/07 5:39PM
0 comments

"Silently we commune, listening rapturously to the
Mournful call of this numinous voice, bearing witness
To hope, light as the feathers that carried
It to this decadent city of the Confederacy."
7/26/07 5:40PM
<u>0 comments</u>

"The loss became another pin-prick ..."
7/26/07 5:41PM
<u>0 comments</u>

"From home
Grown chaos he had fled to wilds, where he
Found comfort and safety beneath its soothing
Blanket."
7/26/07 5:42PM
<u>0 comments</u>

"On the boundaries of this existence
He can still feel those knobby arms
That held him ..."
7/26/07 5:43PM
<u>0 comments</u>

"Silently we commune, listening rapturously to the
Mournful call of this numinous voice, bearing witness
To hope, light as the feathers that carried
It to this decadent city of the Confederacy."
7/26/07 5:44PM
<u>0 comments</u>

"We have come, as conscientious objectors, filing our appeals
Of grievance through grief, in defense of the sacredness
Of life, one condemned to be snuffed out legally."
7/26/07 5:46PM
<u>0 comments</u>

"Mourning
Publicly, the tenderness in our hearts grows as the
Deadly hour draws near, and yet, this rawness we feel
Is soothed through the concrete scented ointment of
Shared compassion."
7/26/07 5:46PM
<u>0 comments</u>

"Viewed from a human point of view, what protection is there?"
7/26/07 5:48PM
<u>0 comments</u>

"Mourning
Publicly, the tenderness in our hearts grows as the
Deadly hour draws near ..."
7/26/07 5:49PM
<u>0 comments</u>

"The loss became another pin-prick in the
Memory ..."
7/26/07 5:50PM
<u>0 comments</u>

"When the caged came forth, wearing
Introspective miens, one of them looked
Towards his daily focal point,
Outside the chain-link fence and experienced its
Absence as through the lenses of an
Arachnid."
7/26/07 5:50PM
0 comments

"From home
Grown chaos he had fled to wilds …"
7/26/07 5:51PM
0 comments

"From the kitchen comes Joseph, a glass
Of red wine in hand and in his eyes a smile"
7/26/07 5:52PM
0 comments

"Here was
Sanctuary, a place to indulge spiritual
Centeredness, where the fragrance of a
Woodland oasis and chuckling waters
Heal."
7/26/07 5:53PM
0 comments

"Living narrow lives does not come easy.
Where would we be without happenstance?"
7/26/07 5:54PM
1 comments

"leaving mighty pains that hunger
And are soothed and quenched by the
Sweetness of seasonal gifts."
7/26/07 5:54PM
0 comments

"This existence, constrained, is not blessed with
An embarrassment of riches. It is fundamental."
7/26/07 5:55PM
0 comments

"When the phone goes silent, on that voice
Sweet as a love song,"
7/26/07 5:56PM
0 comments

"When the phone goes silent, on that voice
Sweet as a love song,"
7/26/07 5:56PM
0 comments

"The voice is gone, memory kicks in and we
Are saved,"
7/26/07 5:57PM
0 comments

"the wider world is
Closed off with the finality of a vacuum sealed
Door,"
7/26/07 5:58PM
0 comments

"Living narrow lives does not come easy.
Where would we be without happenstance?"
7/26/07 5:59PM
0 comments

TEACHING IN PRISONS

The first thing I learned is that a prison classroom is just a classroom like any other classroom.

The second thing I learned is that it isn't.

TO READ ANTONIN ARTAUD'S "ALL WRITING IS PIGSHIT"

STAND
outside the RISD Library on Benefit Street with back to front door

CROSS
Benefit Street *[look right look left look right again]*

CLIMB
College Street to Prospect

TURN
right and proceed up ramp or steps to Brown University's Rockefeller Library

ENTER
through revolving doors *[to conserve heat]*

PRESENT
identification at security desk

CONSULT
Josiah for Mary Ann Caws' *Manifesto: A Century of Isms*

TRANSCRIBE
Call Number *[CB 427.M287 2001]* &

NOTE
location of available copy / copies

PROCEED
to appropriate floor for circulating copy *[consult list by elevator]*
OR Reference Room *[for use in library only]*

PROCURE
book &

CARRY
to coin/card copier on 1st or 2nd floor

COPY
pages 460-1

RETRIEVE
& fold, roll or otherwise temporarily store pages

RETURN
book to Reference Desk or cart

READ/LEAVE/READ

CONSULT
teacher if confused

THOUGHT

The new interdisciplinarity.

MAHI-MAHI

Caught.
Cooked onshore.
Eaten.

Better than a William Carlos Williams poem.

in ducts, between leaves of books, in nooks

don't hide your poems—
no-one will look
I tell my students
in whom I hide
my secrets

what you give it

you give it everything
every time
you give it everything
you give it everything
every time
you give it everything

TIP

Here's something I do when I have to get up:
I go back to sleep.

ALWAYS THE RIGHT THING TO DO

CRANK UP THE MUSIC!!!!

HOW TO SAY THANKS WHEN YOU MEAN IT BUT DON'T REALLY HAVE TIME RIGHT NOW

Thnaks!

EVERYTHING IS UNLIKELY

Everything is unlikely. Look at going to the bathroom. That's unlikely. And you do it so often. At least four times a day. And sometimes at night too. Sleeping is unlikely. You just conk out. Imagine if you were looking at yourself all those hours. You, hardly daring to breathe, looking at yourself, a great inert heap, hardly breathing, in the dark, and every now & again a gigantic snort. You just get slung down into a pit of sleep. Like those bodies in Pompeii. Then in the morning try to make the pieces flow again. Eating is very unlikely. When it comes down to it—what is it but opening your mouth & putting food in? It's not called a cake-hole for nothing. Mysterious chute. My whole life is unlikely. What is America? Why am I here? What happened to the other country? Where did my sisters' houses go? Why am I here—in this house—in this world—which also holds a man screaming as other men saw at his neck with an inadequate knife?

REALITY IS NOT LIKE ITSELF

Reality is not like itself. My daughter says: *I can't believe we have a real live **animal** in our house!* I think of all the life teeming between floorboards, in heating ducts, under eaves, in the basement, in closets, between folds of comforters and skin. All those perfect systems. The centipede in its skein of dark slung beneath every sliver of brightness in our house. The furry heads of bats under the eaves, asleep during our day and ready to leave, before I even know they are there. The bullish complacence of the dust-mite. Or the long-legged spider in the basement of our house inquiring: *Do you believe in an upstairs? I can't believe that there are **humans** in our house!* And the two of us—in some ways as out of place as the lost fly which stumbles in through the mail-slot, or our lonely cat racing from window to window, aghast & electric, chasing birds, dogs, & feral cats with a house in between—lumbering through rooms scant of everything except books.

A CERTAIN CHARM

Reality has a certain charm. It's really happening. Your breast is being stretched & pulled like dough. It's being flattened between two parts of a machine you're afraid to look at. You'd rather chat to the technician who says *A little more? A little more?* And you say *Okay* until you say *That's enough*. There is no anticipation. It's all now. The light is dim. The temperature is so perfect it's almost slimy. A friendly stranger is manipulating your breast like gum. You inhabit each moment as if it were the base of your very own coconut tree, with your very own pallet & suncream. You are packed into that moment like an embryo in the womb. In the cubicle putting your clothes back on, you might feel ugly. You might feel relieved. You might walk out through the glass doors feeling suave, even cracking a joke. You might sit in your car for a minute thinking *Boy I can drive! I'm gonna drive right back into my life*. And you do, re-entering your living-room like a space capsule splash-down. You exit through the hatch into the stage-set of your home. Small shiny actors run towards you. Nothing seems real. Then sooner or later something really strange happens. Six firemen are standing in huge clothes in your upstairs hallway staring at a beeping alarm. *Now this is real*. It's 3am. It's really happening. A man's large hand reaches out & plucks the carbon monoxide alarm off the wall. You're inhabiting each moment again.

WORDS CHUNKS OVER PARKING LOT

Laurie Anderson is speaking in the parking lot. She is on a podium, wearing a velvet hat. Her face shines between the hat & a black refrigerator-shaped robe. Other small faces shine towards hers— faces of women & men, like lenses, terraced on the podium. In the parking lot, thousands of people are listening. Their eyes, ears, brains, even the palms of their hands, are open. *Ten years ago,* says Laurie Anderson. *And now: one in every hundred Americans is in prison.* Her voice laps towards us from her faraway face. The parking lot becomes greyer, realer. It is like that moment when you come out of the water & you realize you are cold. In the air above us, protruding from the radiant sky & latched, like Trotsky's ice-pick, into our breathing-space, the gigantic word: WAR. And tumbled beside it: PRIVATIZATION. And of course PRISON SYSTEM. Above the warm crowns of our heads an impending furniture which calls for walls, & a roof.

THIEF IN THE NIGHT

This morning I found a camera. On the kitchen table. The kitchen table in the dining room. It was a Canon. In a black case. That was what spooked me. Oh we have cameras alright—but not in cases. It must have been a robber. A thief in the night. A weird & troubled robber who documented his own crimes. Who was interrupted— that time I got up to go to the bathroom maybe—and broke off his dastardly doings & fled. It was the only explanation. I looked at the little black lump huddled on the table end. Then I asked my daughter: *Is that your camera?* And she said: *Yes.*

JANUARY

The weather is hot because it has all the old weathers rolled up inside it like laundry. January is stuffed with old Januaries, snowy & chill, but also Februaries & Marches & Aprils & Mays, some of them mild & breathing with a close-to-human warmth. Steam rises from this ball of months, flapping, dismantling, with January panting on top of them, trying to keep them contained. The cherry blossom blossoms, consummately stupid, consummately beautiful. It will not have another chance. It inhabits this warm spell impeccably, as confidently as if it were spring. Or maybe it is we who are stupid, ranting & agreeing to everything, without being consulted & without making our wishes known, because people who make decisions are seen as distant as the sky.

CAT HAIR

I have had my cat for 4 years. It is a big black fat cat now. I reckon I have inhaled multitudinous ever-expanding versions of it over the years. The house is covered in cat hair. Fine falls are let down every day. Some in long black hairs, arced like a bow. Some in rectangular tufts, soft as down though somehow malignant, like a rabbit foot without bones. Some in tumbleweeds, elaborate lattices with presence but no reason. Wiry whiskers like poison darts. I've had to shelve many pressing projects just to deal with it. I'm down on my hands & knees every day, brooding on the cost & whereabouts of the most powerful vacuum cleaner in the world. I can imagine all that cat hair in the pipes of the powerful vacuum cleaner. I can imagine it because I feel all that cat hair inside me, in my own pipes. But it's not the cat hair I see that is the utmost source of my anxiety. Nor the cat hair I miss which, if gathered, could be swathed into an immense bonnet, plus robes. No, it is the cat hair that is too fine to see which provokes my bitterest unease. The cat hair from which color & size have leached. Which swirls through the air I breathe, softly breaching my orifices, nuzzling like optical fibers through my systems, so many cats' eyes in the steamy, uncosmeticized gridwork within, occluded from mine eyes.

A COW

If a cow eats a fridge a bulky object is lodged in its neck which is also broad & oblong like a fridge. A fridge set at angles to a fridge. Or in or within a fridge. Though in fact the neck is more like a dried-blood rug drug across a fridge, awkwardly. The pure idea is that of a crane from which a crate swings at the docks, seagulls strewn like fingernail clippings in the sky behind—noisy slivers like steel shavings tossed in front of the wild blinding sun.

A HERD OF SMALL CATTLE

A bundle of tiny cows comes out every morning before dawn. They puddle around in the dark, I see the flash of their flanks, udders, as they turn. The dry sound of their hooves, like cork. Smell the vivid sweet smell of them. After a while, as it lightens, their speckled flanks jump into focus, down to the freckle. All this happens in my bedroom. Outside is no meadow with sweet grass, just city grime. My city is not a grand one. It is a mean one, though it has its grandnesses, its own speckled flanks and profligate sky. My cows are tiny and not quite real. They are shiny and neat, like cows in manuscripts. They smell like vellum. It is my job to milk them, which I do, in the metallic morning, the hot jet of their milk searing like lemon juice past my clunky, game fingers, into the metallic pail.

TOE & FAUCET

Lying in tub tonight long, long time. Water luke-warm. Need heater-upper. Hand ready to go (want soap anyway). Head says *No, let foot have go*. Toes? Little buggers mad excited in face of mighty task. Up goes foot against faucet. Hand, head, even soap agog. Beautiful! Long old Left Foot laid like fish on faucet. Leaning, Turning. Big Toe exerting pressure. Like tug-of-war but other way. All toes go wild but Big Toe hero of the hour, yessir. Push. Press. Like opening canal lock. Or submarine door. Bit by bit faucet yields. Then gush. Water flow! Tub heats up but what moot point! All talk was Big Toe. But could he shut off? Eyes drill on Left Foot. Watch him lean & grunt again. Shut it down. Shut it down. To thin spool. To drip. To complete removal of wet! Like dry *Pamper*. Then Head gets smart. Sends Foot after soap. But Hand, dolphin of loyalty, shoots out & scoops: *No-one gonna humiliate my man Toe*. Then writes this.

THE AZORES OF TOES

On the great flat sheet of the beach almost like a bed flat sheet in fact, the toes disport, comport themselves looking for all the world like waves of headstones in a perhaps military cemetery except with sunglasses, Aviators probably, given the military issue. The male toes are cool in their Aviators and bare-chested, sporting only swimming trunks. I was never a fan of Aviators for the ladies but fetishes and inhibitions are sprouting like cauliflowers round me at this stage so don't mind me. The tots are the best, I mean toes are small so toe tots just about disappear (through binoculars from the slopes of Pico which is our vantage point) were it not for the puffs of sand they squirt up as they race about and disappear into all over this surfside arena stretched and marked with broad striped beach towels the bright colors of which make the scene a festival. That and the Latin music. If you've never seen a big toe belly-dance you haven't lived. Of course I mean *chamarrita, larum-tum-tum,* and *pezinho.* But the great thing about toes you know is how completely silent they are. You hear the music of course. Then the toes like giant erasers rubbing it out.

GRANNY SMITH APPLES

Granny Smith apples are called Granny Smith apples because there was once a little woman called Granny Smith who had two green eyes like apples, two bright green eyes twinkling in her head. Actually they were out on stalks. No, I'm a liar. It was the stalks were out—like a single stiff eye-lash, like an—the apples were in her head. Another coincidence was that her name at one time was actually Granny Smith Apples but she got married & shortened it because it would have been too long otherwise, for the children. Of course they were the apple of her eye (each one was a segment of the apple & her eyes were apples; they were the apple of her apples therefore the same logic applies). She wasn't that little either, Granny Smith, but kind of large & scary, with those twinkling green eyes, & motey stalks.

AN UNFORTUNATE LIFE

Poor Dot had an unfortunate life. She had no luck. When she was a kid, she spent all her time at school. Then when she left school, she had to work. She saved like a dog & bought a house. Then after 20 years there was a problem with the foundation. She got married; then just before their 40th anniversary her husband died. She had only just retired when her parents died. Another person would have crumbled but she kept going. She bought a condo but it was too small for any of her 6 children—or their children—to stay over. She had to make do with friends & a strange fellow that was always imposing on her & the library & of course the cat. There was no rest for her. She had to drive herself around everywhere, even when she went abroad. She lived 30 years like that, after retirement. But she got sick in the end. I guess she just gave up.

CHILDHOOD MEMORY

I wake up and the bunk bed is made of water. The tubular steel supports are bright cords of water. I slide down like a fireman except there is no red or yellow, no helmet, no stiff flaring jacket, no sound except for the rushing water. I walk through the door & the landing is also water, like one of those moving walkways in airports I realize now, but deep & clear & churned by the commotion of movement. I slip down the waterfall stairs clutching at each step for the water banisters & missing. I'm falling safely but terrified. Then I'm standing in the hall facing the white door of the sitting-room. Water runs in sheets all over the door & the walls of the hall & the beveled glass door of the kitchen & the terrazzo floor are all rushing away from me. The door of the sitting-room will not winnow into transparency. I put out my hand & push & the door backs away & the sitting-room is delivered to me, a slice, an arc, a wobbly 360° and the white faces of my father & mother & the visitors slowly turning. They look like walruses. Supper is spread on a gold and black trolley. The coiled wire element of the electric fire is bright orange with heat. The doctor comes. I lie on the couch & things begin to dry up. My mother mops up the puddles. I see that the house is not made of water but death.

CHILDHOOD MEMORY 2

I am walking home from school at lunchtime. It is Friday. Two days before I was cycling. On that day, Wednesday, lunchtime, I saw a nun and a girl in uniform go into my friend's house, which is the first house on our street. The blazer has broad blue stripes, in royal blue and sky blue. It is the uniform of my friend's school. On Wednesday after school, another friend, 13, though middle-aged, at the corner store, shiny with news: *10 feet in the air, bike, drunk driver, Mater hospital, lunch-time.* But on Friday at lunchtime I am walking home. As I draw close I walk more and more slowly. The curtains of the houses will say so. They will be open, like every time I have come home since Wednesday, or they will be closed. The curtains are closed. I walk past each house to my house and go in. My mother puts dinner on the table. It is fried potatoes. What was my mother thinking—*What do I say now? Best just get on with it.* Slowly I eat my potatoes.

FAMOUS IN YOUR HEAD

You can be very famous in your own head for something. Gilding, for example. Forgery. I am a forger *par excellence*, according to my own legend. I am a master portraitist of Joe Stalin. I am a cunning maker of small cavemen. I am most famous in my head for falling out of boats in Bray and the Sea of Marmara & laughing my head off— that very same head I'm famous in. I'm also famous in my family for cooking & baking & lightning changes of mood. My mother was famous for baking & a red dress. My sister was famous for trickery. They're all gone now, those famous folk. My head is a very small arena but I'm the star there, when the lights are on.

SHORT MOVIE

The guy sitting beside me in the plane plucks the phone from the back of the seat in front & hands it to me telling me to call my hotel to get them to change the room reservations for the Deputy Head of Homeland Security about to check in.

I tell him I don't have a hotel. I'm a college teacher. He says *Well change a grade then* & shoves the phone in my face. I call the Division of Liberal Arts. Gail says I need to fill out a form and drop it over to the Registrar's Office.

In the few seconds it takes to hang up, the last time a grade was forced on me flashes before my eyes. It was at the University of Mississippi, where the clerk at the Registrar's Office window insisted I follow procedure by giving an F to a student who hadn't shown up all semester & probably thought she had dropped the course. I didn't want to do it but then it was pointed out to me that I was holding up the line. All the other teachers standing waiting, semester over, completed grade-sheets in hand.

Now here was this jerk beside me trying to force a grade on me again. I pulled out my pen & drove it into his neck.

HANDSHAKE

A woman holds out her hand to shake. Instead of fingers she has
pens. The pens are articulated in joints so they rattle. They are a lot
like fingers but stiffer & more jolly somehow. She shoots her hand
into the fleshy competent hand of the man she is greeting. He is
astonished by the whirr of pens & the unexpected feel of this glittery
handshake. Pens are, after all, quite a bit thinner than fingers. He is
amazed & repulsed but repulsion wins out, having more exercised
his expressive armory to date. He flings the pen-hand from him,
flattening his suit flap with one clammy downward palm-stroke.
Ink rushes to the pen-fingertips. The woman feels an unbearable
pressure to write.

DEAR DAVE

A woman sits in a restaurant sipping a consommé of loneliness. She is seated at a small table, white & round like a spool of cotton. A flotilla of such tables radiates from her, cross-hatching the dining room floor, as if set up for an elaborate game. In the background: a plate glass window, opening on sea & sky. In the foreground: pot plants. Down right: a slurping. A man is eating a bowl of soup. Impossible to feel lonely while eating minestrone! Baby pasta shells, cherubic, wink up at him, swirling their limpid broth. Kidney beans jump like porpoises out of the mucilage, hurling themselves chinward, skimming parmesan floes where thumbnails of slick onion loll & bask. Cubed parsnips & carrots rattle like bracelets against the portcullis of his teeth. The jaws crank open & the spoon like a zeppelin arrives to pitch load after load of spinach across the fleshy threshold of lip. Inside all is mayhem. The fat tongue disciplines & punishes, stripping sweet peas of their papery skins & pasting their innards against the ridged roof of the mouth. The diced vegetables fight back. Fanned into flying columns, kamikaze morsels attack, downriding draughts of saliva to plant deep into tender mucosa javelin & barb. Piranha peppers dart into gum, pocking, scooping butterballs of tissue out. The man grunts. All the apparatus of his mouth is unfolding, dismantling. The man is eating a live minestrone. The minestrone is eating the man. He is chewing his own head, reddening, gushing tomatoes & blood. Steaming pink waves wash back, capsizing tables, rushing urgently to break, panting, against a pair of neat feet side-by-side beneath a white table on which floats a bone china bowl from which spoon-by-spoon a woman is sipping a consommé of loneliness.

ANOTHER LETTER

This morning I received a letter from myself saying I was not happy. I was concerned. Why on earth was I not happy? What had happened? I racked my brains. Nothing had changed. If anything, things had gotten better. A little voice in the back of my brain began *Well some people are never ...* but I quenched it smartly, like grinding a cigarette out just before doing something you're looking forward to. It was a wonderful night, full of the promise of autumn, the scattered sparks of the cigarette like miniature coals—or fireflies—or foliage— in the thick dusk & the stars just sharpening into cold. Perhaps this letter warranted a phonecall? But I didn't feel up to it. I avoid phone calls whenever possible. I know that about myself. And so, heavy-hearted, I went back inside, sat down at the kitchen table, drew out my pen. *Dear Mairéad—*

GONE

If a thing is not there it is just not there. It is not hiding around the corner from itself. It has not shrunk. It is not crouching inside its own invisibility, giggling or holding its breath. No matter how recently you touched it, your fingertips cannot summon it again. You cannot rewind to the time the thing was there. You cannot lift yourself up & place yourself down in that safe time. When a thing is not there it may or may not be somewhere else but from your kingdom it is gone. Believe your eyes.

TIME

These small poems are made of very pure time. They are small muscles of time.

Email time is a brushed nylon sheet, irritating & stretched thin. Or maybe fibreglass.

When I go to bed early, time is a smooth table, with the prospect of music, books, poems, sleep, hovering like blimps above it. Sitting on the doorstep of sleep is the greatest luxury. The sun always shines in that country. The stoop is so bleached with it, it is made of sun.

Punctuation is a wonderful form of time, stabilizing & reassuring.

When concentrating on one thing, time can be a short life-time, though with the fear & surety of reincarnation.

Mostly time is money. It is gone as soon as pay-day comes, & usually before.

My life is full of roads that go nowhere, train-tracks that abruptly halt. I am left standing on the purple gravel where it plunges into heavy undergrowth. Or testing the weight of short sections of track where without a word they stop.

THE SECRET OF LIFE

Bob Marley

ANOTHER SECRET

Jazz

A FRENCH SECRET

Erik Satie

THE FIRST INTERNET

Louis Armstrong

pops

minstrel

god

wynton

won
duke
ellington's
pulitzer
prize
well
duke did
enough
to win
999
so all
wynton
had to do
was love
duke
& win

1

HEAVEN

I'm in heaven
& God springs
a surprise
party:
it's John Lennon,
Bob Dylan
& Bob Marley.
Someone says
Hey God
Dylan's not dead
& God says
Hey man
this is Heaven.

2005

September
lets me hold her hand briefly
before slipping away

2005—
let me look at
your bright face

even as your slim shoulder
is turning away

ACKNOWLEDGMENTS

Poems in this collection were previously published in the chapbooks
An Educated Heart (Palm Press 2005), *Kalends* (Belladonna* 2005), and
State House Calendar (watersign press/Calendar Girl Books for the Dusie
Kollektiv 2009).

"Spring" was previously published in the collection *SOS Poetry* (/ubu
Editions 2007). "Donald Hall Would Hate Me" is collected in *poem, home:
An Anthology of Ars Poetica* (Paper Kite Press 2009). "Applause" is included
in my talk "Some Differences Between Poetry & Standup" (UbuWeb 2005).
"To Read Antonin Artaud's 'All Writing Is Pigshit'" is included in my
essay "Avant-Garde Pronouns" (*Avant-Post: The Avant-Garde in the Era of
Post-Ideology*, Litteraria Pragensia, 2006).

Other poems were published in the *Argotist Online, Baltimore Is Reads, The
Big Bridge, Cannot Exist, The Drunken Boat, Poetry Salzburg, RealPoetik*, and
Veer.

A warm thank you to the editors of these publications.

The text of "To Skin a Muskrat," "To Skin a Raccoon," "Boarding Beaver,"
and "Fleshing Skunk," except for the final sentence of each, was taken
from www.mntrappers.com. The text of "Provenance," "Of," "Pastimes,"
and "Work," was taken from obituaries in the *Providence Journal*, 2004.
"Another Old Man of Barcelona" is adapted from *Gaudí Obra Completa /
Complete Work Gaudí*, Aurora Cuito, Cristina Montes (Feierabend Verlag
Ohg 2003). The elements of "Puttenham's Forms for Pattern Poetry" are
taken from Dick Higgins' *Pattern Poetry: Guide to an Unknown Literature*
(State University of New York Press, 1987), p.111. Text in "Letters from
Joe Oliver" is from the letters of great jazzman, cornet player, composer
and band leader Joe "King" Oliver to his sister, toward the end of his life.
"Red Skeleton Interviews Nerve Ends, Filaments, & an Electrolyte" and
"Red Skelton Interviews Joseph the Carpenter" were written for Dan Cof-
fey. "Dear Dave" was amended in response to a blog comment by Dave
Bonta. "She in the Bios of 21 Iraqi Poets" and "He in the Bios of 21 Iraqi
Poets" are erasures of the bios accompanying the feature "Twenty One
Iraqi Poets," *Masthead* 9 www.masthead.net.au.

"Baghdad," "Trapped," Rubble," "Broken," "Metaphors, Simile," and "An Almost Welcome Splash of Color" are collage poems, assembled from phrases copied and pasted from Internet coverage of the invasion of Iraq, March/April 2003. "Almost" amends headlines from http://att.net. "Unopened Email, and "Choose Your Husband" are also found poems. The translations which comprise "An Educated Heart" were contributed by members of the Rhode Island School of Design and Providence communities.

Text in "For the Drum Major" is from Dr. Martin Luther King, Jr's sermon "The Drum Major Instinct." Al Giordano described Brad Will as "a thoughtful and serious anarchist" in a report on his death published in the *ACTivist* magazine, October 29th, 2006; the other elements of the poem are taken from breaking Internet news. "Live Lines" is from Darrell Grayson's chapbook *Holman's House*; I tried to make a post each minute in the 30 minutes leading up to the scheduled time of his execution at Holman Correctional Facility, Alabama, on July 26th, 2007.

With grateful acknowledgment to all these writers.

A whole crowd of thanks, a storm of shout-outs to Adam Robinson.

All work was first published on *Heaven* maireadbyrne.blogspot.com

Mairéad Byrne emigrated from Ireland to the United States in 1994, for poetry. Her books include *Talk Poetry* (Miami University Press 2007), *SOS Poetry* (/ubu Editions 2007), and *Nelson & The Huruburu Bird* (Wild Honey Press 2003). She lives in Providence and teaches at Rhode Island School of Design.